WWW.SUPERCHARGEDFINANCE.COM

Introduction to

PERSONAL EFFECTIVENESS

For CFOs and Finance Professionals

CORE SOFT SKILLS AND HOW TO DEVELOP THEM

Andy Burrows

Copyright © 2019 Andy Burrows

All rights reserved, including right of reproduction in whole or in part, in any form.

ISBN 9781678550899

AN INTRODUCTION TO PERSONAL EFFECTIVENESS FOR CFOS AND FINANCE PROFESSIONALS

Core Soft Skills and How to Develop Them

By Andy Burrows

CONTENTS

Introduction 7

Finance Leadership and Influence Starts With This One Simple Thing 11

Setting the Destination and Direction - a Big CFO Skill 21

The Best Finance Leaders Choose Important Over Urgent 31

Relationship Building Skills for Finance Business Partners 41

Great CFOs Listen Without Prejudice 53

Everyone's a Winner with Good Finance Business Partnering 61

Synergies Are Not Cost Savings for the Best CFOs 69

Happy and Effective CFOs Take Care of Themselves 77

About the Author 87

INTRODUCTION

The basis for this book is a series of articles that I first published on the Supercharged Finance blog[1] during 2019. I've had to edit them a little bit for inclusion in the book, but essentially they represent the same ideas.

The series arose out of a reading project that I undertook in order to get a well rounded view of CFO and Finance business partnering roles, and the skills and behaviours involved. And I think it's only fair to acknowledge the influence of at least some of the books I read.

In fact, I'll mention just two of the books, because these are the most relevant to the subject matter presented here.

---

[1] www.superchargedfinance.com

Firstly, a kindle-only book by Alan Warner, _Finance Business Partnering - The search for value,_ was useful in formulating a framework of skills and behaviours for Finance business partnering. Warner's analysis is where I got the three categories that I now talk about - Business acumen, Behavioural, and Technical (although I most commonly call this "Tools and Techniques").

What I quickly realised, and explained in another blog article[2], is that, "CFO skills are essentially well-developed Finance business partner skills. And conversely, Finance business partner skills are developing Chief Financial Officer skills."

CFO skills are on the same continuum as Finance business partnering skills.

That doesn't mean the skills under the three headings are only appropriate for those with a role title of _Finance Business Partner._ They represent critical skills for _all_ those wanting to develop into senior roles within Finance.

And that's why I've started to talk about these three categories as relating to what I call "business-focused Finance" and "Finance leadership".

Secondly, Stephen Covey's masterpiece, _The 7 Habits of Highly Effective People - Powerful lessons in personal change,_ had an enormous impact on me. I've been aware of the book's existence since the mid-90s, and now I'm so disappointed that it took me 20 years to get around to reading it!

---

[2] https://www.superchargedfinance.com/blog/finance-business-partner-best-route-to-cfo-role

Part of the reason for its impact on me was the way that it tied in with what I'd taken away from a leadership development programme I attended in 2004/5 when I worked at Centrica plc. That programme was a real eye-opener for me. And therefore, when I read similar insights in *The 7 Habits* it resonated very strongly.

The other reason that *The 7 Habits* is, in my view, in a league of its own, in terms of the personal improvement genre, is that it steers away from quick fixes and simplistic techniques.

Instead, Covey goes for principles-based character work. And that is, I think, why the book is sometimes misunderstood.

My book is about "personal effectiveness", and as such it focuses on core aspects within the Behavioural category in my business-focused Finance skills framework.

And I have no embarrassment in saying that the chapters within this book are based on Covey's *7 Habits*. What I'm really seeking to do is to reiterate the wisdom in my own words, in a brief way, and directed towards application to Finance professionals and leaders.

What I'm trying to demonstrate in this book is that if you want to progress in your career in Finance, in fact if you want to grow and achieve more, then these common-sense behaviours must become increasingly prevalent in the way you live and work.

And, in fact, without these "personal effectiveness" habits gluing everything together, the other skills we talk about in Finance and business leadership become merely a random ragbag of techniques.

My online training venture, Supercharged Finance[3], is all about is developing accountants and Finance professionals to become wise and shrewd business leaders, such as CFOs and CEOs.

That involves growing in every area to become *business-focused* Finance professionals. And the core enablers and accelerators of that growth are the habits and behaviours of "personal effectiveness".

And even though this is admittedly only a brief overview, I hope that these chapters provide you with an entry point into deep thinking that will spark your energy and growth as a Finance professional.

And I hope, perhaps, that you'll one day trace a critical moment in your Finance leadership career back to this point.

Andy Burrows, December 2019

---

[3] www.superchargedfinance.com

FINANCE LEADERSHIP AND INFLUENCE STARTS WITH THIS ONE SIMPLE THING

What you are reading, whether you realise it now or not, could lead to a turning point in your career. And I'm confident that I'm not overstating the case.

What I want to talk about is something that I learnt that revolutionised my thinking about 15 years ago.

I hope that I manage to get this across clearly to you, because the things I'm going to talk about can:

- Be a foundation for growth in your career;
- Start to give you the confidence to do bigger things and make quicker progress;
- Give you the ability to build new and more productive habits.

So, I hope that I manage to spark something important for you here in this short chapter in the same way that someone did for me during a 3-day leadership programme 15 years ago.

ARE YOU STUCK AS A FINANCE BUSINESS PARTNER OR CFO?

So, let's first consider where you are now.

Do you find yourself complaining that you can't do much Finance business partnering (even as a CFO) because of all the mundane 'stuff' you have to do? Do you feel like your working days are filled with keeping on top of emails, grinding out numbers, writing commentaries, reconciling figures, answering stupid questions, doing endless budget iterations that don't make any difference, etc etc?

Are you a Chief Financial Officer, or in senior Finance leadership, and you're finding it difficult to gain any influence? Do people find it easy to dismiss whatever you say? Do they roll their eyes and talk behind your back about you being a "bean counter"? And yet, I bet you're also one of the ones who gets the blame when things go wrong!

And then on top of that you see other Finance business partners, CFOs, Finance leaders, out there making a difference, talking positively, engaging well with the business, trusted and valued.

You're thinking, "those people prove it must be possible. But how can I do that? It feels beyond me! I just don't have the time. There's no one to support me."

And even someone like me – how did I go from being a 'bog-standard' accountant (in 1995) to a regular Finance writer and an "influencer" in the CFO and Finance leadership space, an author and internet entrepreneur... without giving up along the way because of four redundancies and four rounds with cancer (one of which I'm still going through as at the time of writing!)?

THERE'S NO OVERNIGHT SUCCESS IN FINANCE LEADERSHIP

The first thing to say about myself, and literally everyone who is doing well in Finance business partnering and Finance leadership, whether they publicly talk about it or not, is that there was no way to get where we've got in one simple step overnight.

There is no magic.

But there *is* a 'secret sauce' that we keep neglecting to talk about!...

It's not all about circumstance. We haven't had lucky breaks. It's not simply that we've had the good fortune to work in great companies. It's not random.

What I have to talk to you about today is the first, foundational, aspect of the core skillset you need to make progress as a Finance business partner, CFO or in any Finance leadership role.

PERSONAL EFFECTIVENESS IN FINANCE LEADERSHIP

And, so you know, I'm choosing my words carefully. I say that you need this skillset to "make progress" and not to "be successful". Not only is success subjective and relative, it's not entirely within your control.

We should never beat ourselves up or give up because we don't achieve some particular goal. The most important things are growth and progress.

Conversely, whilst it's rightly satisfying to celebrate success in achieving something, we also need the wisdom to be humble and recognise it wasn't all down to our superiority in anything, and to celebrate more the way that we went about it and what we learnt.

Ok, no more preamble! Let's get to the point!

The 'secret sauce' skillset I'm talking about is what I would call "personal effectiveness".

If you've read my blog article on the areas of skill needed to be a Finance business partner or CFO[4], you'll know that I categorise the skills needed for Finance leadership under three headings – Business Acumen, Behavioural and Tools/Techniques.

Personal effectiveness is within the "Behavioural" category. In fact, it's the fundamental subset, the linchpin, the gasoline that ignites the others.

At the risk of getting repetitive, quoting from that article: "In my 25-year career in accountancy and finance, I can honestly say that what I've learnt in this [behavioural skills] area has been more helpful, more revolutionary, more career- and life-propelling, than any technical area. These are skills that not only help you at work, but will help you in every area of life, in marriage and relationships and friendships."

---

[4] https://www.superchargedfinance.com/blog/cfo-skills

WHY START WITH PERSONAL EFFECTIVENESS AS A FINANCE BUSINESS PARTNER?

The reason I see this as so important is that fundamentally Finance business partners, Chief Financial Officers and Finance leaders are called to have credibility and influence in the business. They have to (progressively with their experience and seniority) lead the business to perform well.

And if it's all about leading others then you have to start with yourself. People allow themselves to be influenced and led by people with personal credibility.

If you can't lead yourself, how can you lead others?

If you can't get out of the mire of mundane work and lack of reputation yourself then how can you lead others, and lead a business, out of strategic performance problems?

And since research has shown that to become an expert in a complex skill takes 10 years of purposeful practice (see findings quoted by Matthew Syed[5] and Malcolm Gladwell[6]), you need to get a handle on this as soon as you can!

That's why I put this early in the skills development continuum for Finance business partners on the way to CFO roles.

---

[5] *Bounce*

[6] *Outliers*

STUPIDLY SIMPLE WAYS TO BREAK OUT OF A RUT

There are several aspects to the skillset that I called "personal effectiveness". And I'm going to plot through them in this book.

But I'm going to start here with something so simple you may be tempted to dismiss it. I urge you not to!

But first let me give you some illustrations from my own experience.

In May/June 2018 I set myself a challenge. I called it my "30-day LinkedIn Video Challenge".

I publicly committed to posting a short video on LinkedIn every working day for a 30-day period. My intention was to start to train myself to get over my awkwardness on camera especially in unscripted situations.

I was outside my comfort zone and very nervous to start with. By the end of 30 days I was much better and feeling much more relaxed, aided by the fact that people were very kind in their feedback. (And if you're really interested, you can find those videos on the Supercharged Finance YouTube channel.)

Ten years earlier I was outside my comfort zone in a different way.

I was pursuing a business venture that required me to do a lot of networking. The thought scared me... a lot! Perhaps you can relate!

But I asked a little advice, read some simple tips, gave myself a good talking to (that's the important part!) and joined some networking groups. Many nice breakfasts later and I'd formed a load of new relationships and was enjoying regular conversations with small business owners, finding out about what they did.

However, the foundations were laid about three years before that, just after the leadership programme I referred to earlier.

Wanting to apply what I'd learnt in the programme, I committed (to myself) to do something every week that made me nervous. Baby steps. Actually, it didn't even have to make me nervous. It just had to be different to what I would normally do.

So, I sat at a different desk; used a different car park; wore a colourful tie; used phone rather than email; decided to be first to volunteer for exercises at the front of class in training courses or team meetings, or ask the first question in a CEO Q&A session; and so on. It didn't have to make a difference to anything, or even be noticeable to other people, just so long as it was breaking habits.

My aim in this was partly to prove to myself that making changes and doing new things was simply an act of the will. In the past sometimes I'd felt unable to do new things or do things differently. But I had to realise that there were few physical barriers, and that with the right direction and guidance change is possible... and in many cases much easier than you think.

After a while, the changes were more noticeable and more nerve-wracking. But my fear level was decreasing as I realised that nothing bad happened when I changed things!

FINANCE LEADERSHIP SKILLS ARE WITHIN YOUR REACH

I hope you'd agree that the last example is something that you could do.

And it's based on a skill I'm calling a "can-do attitude"!

Henry Ford famously said that, "whether you think you can or think you can't, you're right!" I used to annoy my team with that one as a Finance Director even before that leadership programme I was talking about! I also wasn't very popular for telling the team that, "where there's a will there's a way!"

But this is the essence of this incredible insight!

The people you see who make great progress with things, who don't give up, who overcome adversity, who over time develop amazing gravitas and credibility, are the people who have this outlook either naturally or with intentional development.

You may dismiss this as just one random element and think that it's ok for you to continue with the "Eeyore" negative mentality!

But my realisation at that leadership programme 15 years ago was that this is backed by research, and in reality, it's the starting point and foundation for great leadership via personal effectiveness.

FIRST PERSONAL EFFECTIVENESS SKILLS AS A FINANCE BUSINESS PARTNER

This has been quite a long chapter, because it's a really important topic. But I just want to finish with three very simple concepts that underpin the "can-do attitude". There's more to it, of course, but if you write these down and think about them, I'm sure you will start to experience some growth.

1. We are not animals. We are not governed by any kind of determinism that says that our response to stimuli is inevitable. There is a gap between stimulus and response where we all have the ability to choose. We are "response-able", as Stephen Covey says in probably one of the best books I have ever read – *The 7 Habits of Highly Effective People*.

We are able to move our thinking from, "I *have to* do xyz", to, "I *choose to* do xyz."

2. Give yourself a good talking to! When we are in that gap between stimulus and response (often we deliberately imagine ourselves there in order to think it through), we can ask ourselves why (normally subconsciously) we find ourselves inclined to a particular course of action.

We are blessed, as human beings, set apart from animals, with self-awareness, imagination, conscience and free will, amongst other things. We can analyse our motives and intentions. And what we find is that quite often our normal inclination is based on false beliefs (such as, "everyone will laugh at me if I speak on a stage").

If we can consciously challenge the false beliefs underpinning the way we normally respond, we find we are able to change our inclination very quickly to the exact opposite! This is what I meant by, "giving myself a good talking to."

3. Keeping commitments. Making small commitments and sticking to them consistently will build new habits and replace old ways of doing things.

NOW OVER TO YOU

Now it's time for you to start. Why not choose the next 30 days to change something, something not too difficult, make a commitment and stick to it consistently? And then reflect on how your "can do attitude" has gone up a level.

SETTING THE DESTINATION AND DIRECTION - A BIG CFO SKILL

I'd like you come away from this chapter knowing how to get a clearer or renewed sense of direction.

Not only that, but I hope that you will have learnt some insights into how you can assess and define the direction you want to go in both your life and work.

Clearly, I write to Finance people, and I'm addressing this to those who are somewhere on the continuum between Finance business partner and CFO or who want to embark on that journey. However, I'm going to be talking about principles that can be used in pretty much any walk of life or work.

THE IMPORTANT CONTEXT

Two blog articles form the foundation and context for this book.

In the first, I pointed out that Finance Business Partner is the new best route to a CFO role[7]. In that article I was establishing the need to better define and support one of the most important development pathways post-accountancy.

In the other article I outlined from recent literature and my own research and experience the three areas of skill needed to develop as a Finance business partner into a good CFO[8]. Those three areas are:

- Tools/Techniques
- Business acumen
- Behavioural

So, in embarking on the core subject matter, in the previous chapter I homed in on just one of those skills areas, saying, Finance leadership and influence starts with this one simple thing.

Within the 'Behavioural' category there is (I'm proposing) a critical subcategory focused on what I'd call, "personal effectiveness". You could also call it, "personal leadership". **The point is that if we're eventually working up and out into to leadership skills, let's start by developing our ability to lead ourselves.**

The powerful starting point in that area is the skill of being able to use a "can do attitude" to *choose* to build new habits and *intentionally* grow. And I gave some simple tips to get started.

---

[7] https://www.superchargedfinance.com/blog/finance-business-partner-best-route-to-cfo-role

[8] https://www.superchargedfinance.com/blog/cfo-skills

GREAT CFOS ARE ABOUT DIRECTION AND DESTINATION

This time, having discovered we have the power of choice and can develop our ability to intentionally change and grow, we turn our attention to what guides our choices. This is the skill and discipline of "destination and direction".

And this is the essence of leadership.

Just quickly first, though, why do I say that Finance business partners have to start developing these skills? Two reasons:

It takes 10 years (as I mentioned earlier) to become expert in a complex skill, and that includes leadership. So, it's best to get started as early as possible!

I believe that Finance business partners are called to influence business decisions to a large extent. That, in my view, makes them leaders. And experienced leadership coach, Penny Ferguson, agrees: "Being a leader, in its broadest context, is about recognising that the minute you influence another person you are, in fact, leading." (*Transform Your Life*, p117)

But back to the point!

If we see our actions each day, the actions of our teams and our employers, the businesses we work for, as *moving us* somewhere, *achieving* something, we have a choice. We can either choose where to head or what we try to achieve, or we can just carry on and see where we end up.

Which would you rather do? Choose the destination or wonder where you are when you get there?

Leadership is choosing the direction and destination. (If you want a contrast with management, management is organising the work to effectively follow the direction and get to the destination.)

LEADERS START WITH THEMSELVES

So, let's look at this on a personal level first.

This is important – firstly, because you must become credible in leading yourself before other people will let you lead them.

But, secondly, because to be a great leader you need to develop a habitual way of thinking in terms of direction. The purpose, the destination, the direction, becomes the way you think, the filter you use on every decision.

So, come on then, personally speaking, where are you heading? Where do you want to end up?

Many people will immediately think about their dream house, becoming a CFO (if they're not one already), having lots of money, holidays and things.

But many of these things are so short term. What happens when you get to that destination? Are you seriously going to set another destination, and go through your life aiming to accumulate more and more stuff? What will that look like? Imagine it! Will you be happy? Will your family be happy?

Thinking forward towards the end of your life, long after you've retired, imagine a dinner in your honour. What would be particularly pleasing to hear them say?

"Here's Johnny. He's great! He's got 14 Ferraris and a yacht!"?

Or, "Here's Johnny. He's great! He has such a good heart, always has time for people, and is such an encouragement to people going through illness."?

WHERE DOES YOUR MOTIVATION COME FROM?

Part of what this question does is to make you think about what your values are – the source of your security, your guiding principles, your source of motivation, wisdom and strength.

In other words, the most satisfying goals are about *being*, not *having*. And it turns out they're the most empowering.

Stephen Covey said, "The key to the ability to change is a changeless sense of who you are, what you are about and what you value." (*The 7 Habits of Highly Effective People*, p108).

But here's the thing. There are lots of things that may be functioning at our core to motivate us and affect our sense of security, guidance, wisdom and strength. Even these shouldn't be accepted uncritically.

For example, imagine a woman who gets her security, guidance and strength from her husband. She does everything she can to be what she considers to be a "good wife", even giving up a good job to be there for him and their kids. That's part of her core values, to be a "good wife". And suddenly he lets her down in a big way. That's going to be devastating. So much for security and strength!

Or, for example, imagine someone who is all about "being the best" at their job. They pour all their energy into their job, to the neglect of their family. And then they get laid off. Devastating again.

And in both cases, it's unbalanced.

Unfortunately, I haven't got the time to develop this fully.

But it must be clear by now that this whole area is one where it's worth getting really analytical and intentional. You want to understand where your motivation is coming from, what your core values are, and how they balance in each of the areas of your life...

... and then *decide* what your core values really should be based on.

THE FINANCE BUSINESS PARTNERING DESTINATION

So, let's come back to talking about Finance business partnering skills and Finance leadership.

Finance leaders, CFOs and influencers can apply their "destination and direction" skills in very practical ways.

There's a couple of levels.

Firstly, there's the day-to-day level. This is what my series of articles, *The Purpose-driven CFO*[9], is all about.

It's saying, practically, in everything we do in Finance, let's recognise *why* we're doing things. Let's look at what we're aiming at, and make sure that what we're doing actually gets us there effectively.

---

[9] https://superchargedfinance.com/blog/the-purpose-driven-cfo-why-be-purpose-driven

But secondly, there's our organisational purpose and mission. Rather than leaving this to chance, we should be intentional and explicit about it.

And this means not only does a good CFO get the team to help put together a mission/vision statement for Finance. It also means Finance business partners, Finance leaders and CFOs, knowing about the purpose and mission of each of the business component parts, and the business as a whole.

We should be thinking naturally in terms of purpose, mission, strategy and vision. These should be the bedrock of the insights and influence we provide in the business. And therefore, we should be developing the skills to think in this way – part of our "personal effectiveness" behavioural skills.

THE SKILLS TO SET THE DESTINATION

Just to finish off with, let's think of what the skills actually involve that enable you to think in terms of destination and direction.

The skill of thinking in this way involves being both analytical and doing some visualisation (using your imagination) and creativity.

As trained accountants, we're not usually wired early on to be creative. Some of us are, obviously (I was a musician and songwriter before I was an accountant!). But if we've put a lot of time and effort into learning a load of accounting techniques and facts, then we probably haven't developed thorough creative skills.

Have you heard about "left-brain" and "right-brain" thinking?

Left-brain thinking is very analytical and methodical. Right-brain thinking is thinking in a more holistic way, more creatively and artistically.

Every human being cannot help using both sides, apparently. But, initially as we grow up, some of us develop one side more than the other.

The trick is to get both sides working together. And looking forward, plotting a destination, analysing core values and motivations, and so on, involves applying both analytical and creative skills.

So, in conclusion, if we're going to be effective leaders/influencers, we have to get some practice at being creative, using our imagination (and analysis) skills to look forward and within for the right direction.

Three quick ways you can get the practice you need to become more creative are:

- Writing a daily journal;
- Going somewhere quiet and meditating, visualising something in the future or in a different location;
- Playing brain games, even ones you get on smartphone apps!

WHERE NEXT WITH FINANCE BUSINESS PARTNERING SKILLS?

So, as we're getting into "personal effectiveness" as a Finance business partnering skill area, we've started from the powerful entry point of the "can do attitude" and the skills to effect personal change and build new habits.

Now we've seen that we need to develop creativity and imagination in order to find our motivating forces and think in terms of destination and direction.

In the next chapter, I'll cover the next critical piece of "personal effectiveness".

That is, "focus".

I can't wait! Can you?!

THE BEST FINANCE LEADERS CHOOSE IMPORTANT OVER URGENT

In this book I'm trying to show the power of some key 'soft' skills that Finance business partners should learn, and CFOs should have.

In this chapter, I hope to show you how to make time to focus on what's important.

This is not simply prioritisation. And whilst you may feel that you've heard most of it before, I'm going to finish up by showing you why your prioritisation is probably not working in your daily organisation.

What I've said so far is that the core of the behavioural skills you need is all about "personal effectiveness". If you can't lead yourself personally, how can you lead or influence others as a Finance business partner or CFO?

There is a real difference between *average* Finance business partners and the *high performing, highly effective* Finance business partners and CFOs.

Average Finance business partners continually complain about not having time to do business partnering because they've got too much number crunching to do.

On the other hand, the *highly effective* Finance business partners seem to have no trouble having the right conversations and gaining the confidence of the business without breaking a sweat! They even have time to come on LinkedIn and tell you about their experiences!

And I've been saying that the secret – because I haven't seen many people saying this until now – is in learning the skills that make up "personal effectiveness". That's the starting point.

The first thing you need is the skill of the "can do attitude" – an understanding that you are able to make choices and effect change in your life.

And in the chapter before this one, I went on to talk about the skill of setting destination and direction.

The skill I want to talk about in this chapter is all about being able to take action towards your destination.

COMMON PROBLEMS FOR FINANCE BUSINESS PARTNERS

I mentioned earlier the Finance business partners who complain of not having enough time to do the business partnering part of their job.

And, to be honest, it's a general problem – not having enough time I mean. That's what we find our ourselves saying quite a lot. "I wish I had time for *xyz*!"

But here's the thing. My wife has this one worked out! She says to me, "why didn't you do *xyz*?"

I reply, "Oh, I didn't have time!"

And then she nails it – "it's not that you didn't have time. You just chose to do something else instead!"

That can be quite embarrassing when you chose to play video games rather than do one of the many household jobs that have needed doing for weeks! "Didn't have time", doesn't really come across well then!

But what it shows is that **the challenge isn't really *time* management. It's *self*-management.** Time needs no management. It just happens. What you choose to do in the time, and your efficiency and effectiveness in using time, is the issue.

THE FOUR QUADRANTS

One of the most useful ways to think is in terms of a matrix that looks like this:

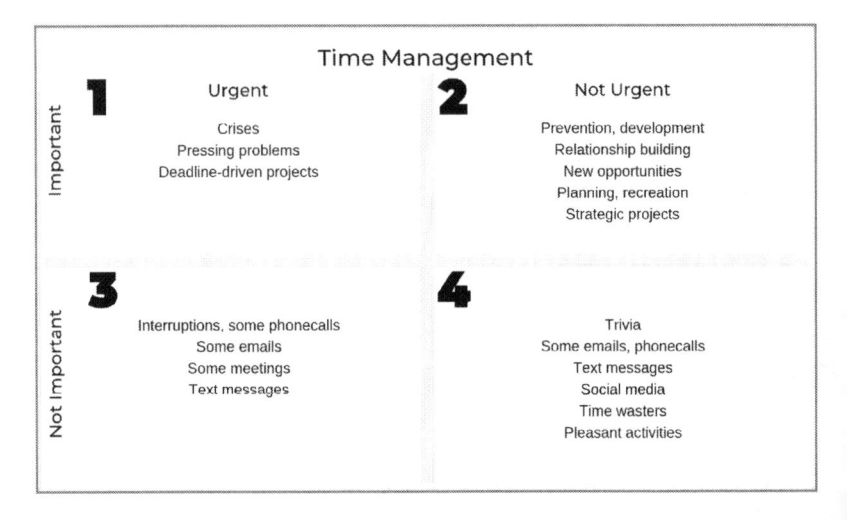

	Urgent	Not Urgent
Important	**1** Crises Pressing problems Deadline-driven projects	**2** Prevention, development Relationship building New opportunities Planning, recreation Strategic projects
Not Important	**3** Interruptions, some phonecalls Some emails Some meetings Text messages	**4** Trivia Some emails, phonecalls Text messages Social media Time wasters Pleasant activities

Time Management

(By the way, this is not an "Eisenhower Matrix". I'm taking this version from Stephen Covey's awesome classic, *The 7 Habits of Highly Effective People*.)

The two factors that can be used to describe an activity are urgency and importance.

Urgent things require immediate attention, whether they're important or not. The person standing at your desk wanting to ask you a question, the phone ringing, some emails, text messages.

Importance, on the other hand, is to do with where it fits with what you're trying to achieve. If something isn't important, it's because it doesn't get you anywhere that you value as a worthwhile destination, when all is said and done, urgent or not.

I think we've all experienced times when we spend most of our time in the first quadrant, where things are urgent *and* important. This is crisis management and, if it isn't rectified, leads to stress, firefighting, more firefighting, and eventually burnout.

When we're predominantly in quadrant 1, we sometimes come out for a break into quadrant 4, because it gives us the feeling of doing stuff without the pressure. We wouldn't dare touch quadrant 2, because it feels too difficult.

Some people spend a lot of time in quadrant 3, thinking they're in quadrant 1! In reality, they're probably just spending a lot of time in other people's meetings, answering text messages, emails and phones in between (and often during the meetings too). They're reactive, letting other people determine their priorities. They don't plan much, and often feel out of control and like a victim.

People who spend their time mainly in quadrants 3 and 4 (i.e. doing unimportant activities) are on the road to nowhere!... or being fired!

Quadrant 2 is the key to effective self-management.

HEARD IT ALL BEFORE?

Unfortunately, I've come across people who seem to think that just because they can use the terminology it means they're being as effective in their self- and team-management as they can. "Yeah I know your project is important to the department, but we need to get through all our urgent and important stuff before we can get to your important non-urgent stuff."

But it doesn't work like that.

Effective people spend *most of their time* intentionally on quadrant 2 activities, and minimise the size and impact of quadrant 1 through good planning and risk management.

That's the point. These activities are not pressing on you. If you're going to do them, you have deliberately start them and deliberately continue and complete them – by choice, and act of independent will!

SCHEDULE IMPORTANT ACTIVITIES INTENTIONALLY

How do effective people schedule their time to make sure they give attention to the much-neglected quadrant 2 (important but not urgent)?

What I've learnt is to spend time at the start of every week planning the week (not just at the start of each day). And, yes, it takes self-discipline to set aside that time. But there are 96 hours in a week when you're not asleep. If you can't find 0.25 to 0.50 of an hour each week to make your week more productive and make yourself more effective, then you might as well give up!!

And there's a two-stage process:

For each of the roles you have in life (wife, mother, manager, individual, netball player, etc), think of two or three important things you want to achieve in the next seven days, and record them as goals.

Schedule time to make progress on them in your planner or calendar, either as appointments or priorities.

Obviously, there are many factors involved in finding appropriate times for various types of quadrant 2 activities. You may need a quiet place for some activities, a phone line for others, the internet for others, just a laptop for others. You may want to minimise travel, or there may be things you can best schedule into travel time (audio books, podcasts, etc).

Thinking about all this in advance makes it more likely you will actually do it.

But you still have to be flexible. Sometimes days don't turn out as planned, and maybe you have to change your schedule. It's not the end of the world.

As Stephen Covey says, "The key is not to prioritize what's on your schedule, but to schedule your priorities."

FROM CRISIS MANAGEMENT TO EFFECTIVE SELF-MANAGEMENT

If you're stuck in the vicious circle of everything being urgent, and you're constantly working long hours with tight deadlines, one idea to break out of the cycle and take control is to identify the quadrant 3 and 4 activities (i.e. non-important) you may be doing. Then you can start to replace that with spending some time focusing on quadrant 2.

As you spend more time on the forward-thinking activities in quadrant 2, the urgent crises of quadrant 1 should become less frequent, and you will spend more of your time achieving the important results you really want to, in keeping with your mission, your values and vision.

But what this really highlights is that in order to do the important things you really feel will make a difference in your life, and in your work, you have to *choose* to say "no" to other activities, which some people may consider urgent (like answering their text messages and phone-calls).

BUT WHY ISN'T IT WORKING?

Well, you can see that this is all common-sense stuff. It's not particular to the Finance audience I regularly address. It's not unique to Finance leadership, CFOs or Finance business partners.

It is a critical skill to learn, though, as Finance professionals, Finance business partners and Finance leaders.

It's not uncommon, however, to be dissatisfied with the results. Maybe you've tried such things and think you've failed? And I think we have a particular lesson to learn here as Finance people.

You see, most people think that if this technique doesn't work well for them, there's a problem with the way they're doing it. Perhaps they lack the self-discipline? Perhaps they are too weak to say "no" to the non-important stuff?

But, in actual fact, it turns out on reflection, to be the fact that what is driving us and motivating us is not strong enough. We have not reflected deeply enough on the values and purpose that give us the motivation that leads to our personal mission – the destination and direction I was talking about in the previous chapter.

And it's the congruence of our weekly goals with our personal mission and values that gives those goals importance to us.

Putting it bluntly, *we simply don't want these things enough!*

And I made the point in that chapter that we need to be self-critical when it comes to our motivation.

For example, if your personal mission is to make your business partners happy, then you're not going to spend much time in quadrant 2, because you're making your goals and priorities depend on the reaction of others. You'll be forever reacting to their needs and spend all of your time in quadrants 1 and 3.

But if you were to rephrase that in terms of *being* a good Finance business partner (the focus here is on you and what you can control, rather than on external responses you can't control), then you'd be able to say "no" to the "urgent" quadrant 3 requests of even your non-Finance contacts so that you can be a better Finance business partner.

The particular lesson I want Finance business partners, CFOs, Finance leaders, in fact anyone in Finance, to learn, however, is to *spend more time on mission, vision, purpose and values* – the destination and direction from the previous chapter.

If we want the power to be able to say "no" to competing priorities and focus on the important, then we need *a "bigger 'yes' burning inside"* (Stephen Covey).

We have to really believe in our principles and our values and the source of our motivation.

And the reason I particularly direct this at Finance leaders is because we're *not very good at it!*

From my experience with CFOs and senior Finance leadership teams, we really do just pay lip service to *purpose, vision* and *mission*.

We assume that because we're accountants we must have been somehow brainwashed by our certifying bodies to know what we're all about in our work in business! Or we write it off as empty "consultant-speak"! Or we roll the eyes in a way that says, "that's namby pamby stuff for people in Marketing or HR. Fine for them. We'll just get on with our work!"

We have to change this culture, and become *purpose-driven*. We have to develop the skill to set the destination and direction, as well as the skill to organise ourselves to follow the direction and reach the destination.

We cannot afford to neglect the 'soft' skills that start with "personal effectiveness" if we want to be good Finance business partners, and to become the great leaders that CFOs are supposed to be!

RELATIONSHIP BUILDING SKILLS FOR FINANCE BUSINESS PARTNERS

In this chapter, I want to talk about relationship-building skills as a Finance business partner. And I want you to come away with tangible ideas as to how you can improve the way you build relationships.

Just to recap, I'm assuming that Finance business partner is the new best route to a CFO role, and you'll remember that in a Supercharged Finance blog article[10] I mapped out the three skills areas that are common throughout the continuum from Finance business partner to CFO.

And what I've done so far in this book, then, is to focus in on one really important subsection of behavioural skills that I believe is the key to all the rest – "personal effectiveness". And I've spent the last three chapters expanding on the foundations.

---

[10] https://www.superchargedfinance.com/blog/cfo-skills

And you may have found it quite weird that I started with skills that are very much individual personal skills. I mean, Finance business partnering is fundamentally all about dealing with other people. And so, you might expect that I'd be focusing on interpersonal skills, like influencing or communication.

But, my argument has been that if you're going to lead others (and influencing is a form of leadership) then you have to start by leading yourself.

If you can't bring about change in your own life and work, where is your credibility to lead others through change and improvement?

So, you have to start with developing a "can do attitude". You have to learn to search into yourself for your motivation, having the ability to critically assess the values and principles you use, and to use creativity and imagination to set a vision and direction. And you have to be able to manage yourself to do the important work of following that direction, while other urgent matters continue to press in on you.

Now I'm going to pivot towards building interpersonal skills onto that foundation.

SEVEN HABITS

I've been basing everything in this series on one of the best books I've ever read: Stephen Covey's _The 7 Habits of Highly Effective People_. I wish I'd read it earlier in my life.

And at the risk of digressing too much, I want to say that a lot of people misunderstand that book. If you really take the time to understand it, it is quite revolutionary. But I've seen too many people make the mistake of thinking Covey's main insight was the whole important vs urgent thing I outlined in the previous chapter (I saw an article in Forbes recently saying exactly that).

And one of the things in the book that very gently presses from beginning to end is Covey's belief that your personal effectiveness increases to the extent that you are living your life (and building your habits) according to "correct principles".

The principles he's talking about are things like fairness, integrity, honesty, human dignity, service, excellence, growth/potential, patience, encouragement.

He makes the point that, "principles are not values. A gang of thieves can share values, but they are a violation of the fundamental principles we're talking about.... Principles are guidelines for human conduct that are proven to have enduring, permanent value. They're fundamental. They're essentially unarguable because they are self-evident." (p35)

FINANCE BUSINESS PARTNERS AND OTHER PEOPLE

And so, as we pivot towards the interpersonal skills, and as we talk about relationship building as a Finance business partner, I want to start by mentioning two unhelpful Finance business partnering stances as examples.

First example – thinking it's all about my influence.

I can't help feeling a little uncomfortable when those working in Finance business partnering describe their aspiration as becoming more influential in business decision making.

My question is, how does that mean we are viewing other people, our non-Finance colleagues?

Are we assuming that we have all the right answers and that we just need to find (hopefully quick) ways of manipulatively persuading and influencing our non-Finance colleagues to accept our viewpoint?

Is that the right way to view influencing? Is that the right way to view other people – just there to be influenced to carry out our ideas?

Second example – going "native", i.e. taking sides with the non-Finance manager you're partnering with and helping them 'beat the system' (that the Finance team controls!)

I've seen this *a lot*! I even discovered one of my direct reports doing it and hiding it from me!

I discovered that the accruals balance was a mish-mash of spurious credits and debits he'd entered in the system, with no backup, to massage the costs of each department to balance to the plan or forecast.

He did this because he saw it as his job to help the corporate cost centre managers "beat the system" and avoid getting their costs cut when they were under budget or getting in trouble when they were over budget! (No wonder the cost centre managers never had a bad word to say about him!)

Even CFOs do this when they tell one story to the CEO, another to the Exec team, and yet another to the shareholders/investors.

But what does that mean? We are manipulating reactions – i.e. trying to get the end results we want (in terms of bonuses, reputation, career longevity, or simply a quiet life!) by means of telling lies with numbers.

ETHICS AND FINANCE BUSINESS PARTNERING?

So, it's time to ask the divisive question – how do *you* want to do the Finance business partnering job? By manipulation, lies and deceit? By politics, semantics and clever presentation of information (i.e. spin)?

Or by using your skills and experience to help your colleagues collaboratively to achieve a common objective – clear improvement in the performance of the business that you can all be proud of together?

In terms of "correct principles", our qualifying accountancy bodies are very clear and upfront, which has always resonated strongly with me. The very first thing you're taught by the ICAEW, and I assume the same of ACCA, CIMA and all the others across the world, is the "code of ethics" – principles such as *objectivity, confidentiality, integrity, professional behaviour, professional competence*.

Please don't get me wrong. I'm not naïve. I've seen these flouted on a monthly basis throughout my career. But I believe in "correct principles" enough not to become cynical.

What I'm doing here is saying that as we pivot from our self-leadership skills to look at relationship-building skills, our principles will determine how we develop.

Do we just want some quick techniques to help us get what we want out of our business colleagues? Or do we want to build skills based on character and principles that will help us relate to everyone better in the long run?

And I say that lest you think that what I say next can be reduced to a set of quick tips and techniques.

FINANCE BUSINESS PARTNERING AND LEADERSHIP BASED ON TRUST

Fundamentally, relationship-building and the positivity and smooth working of relationships is all based on trust. Negotiation, persuasion, communication, all feel so much better when the level of trust is higher.

I'm not going to spend any time proving that. I think it's self-evident.

So, the question is then, how can I build trust so that I experience those benefits when it comes to communication, persuasion and leadership?

And I've got a few ideas to help you make a start. Think of these in your dealings with every person you have any kind of relationship with, and you can start to build up that level of trust that you need. And it's genuine trust, too, because these things will actually make you habitually more trustworthy!

1. UNDERSTAND THE INDIVIDUAL

Everyone is different. We are all different mixes of personality types, emotions, hobbies, family experiences, and so on.

Taking the time to understand 'what makes them tick' is something that builds up trust.

An example of this is the irony of having a conversation focused on the other person. I learnt this when I used to do a lot of networking. You get in conversation with someone, you ask them questions, show a real interest in them and their business… and they go away thinking what a great person you are and what a great conversation they had with you. They possibly start to think of you as someone they can do business with… and you may not have even told them what business you're in!

If you then show that you were listening, by building that understanding of them into your future conversations and activities, you can build even more trust.

2. DON'T NEGLECT THE LITTLE THINGS

Even what we might call "stupid little things" build trust.

I remember working in a very big Finance function. The Group Finance Director could have been excused for not being very visible, since the Finance function had almost 1,000 people.

And yet, he'd regularly come down from the Exec floor on a Friday afternoon just to wander round chatting to people in Finance.

And, more to the point, he would remember the conversations he had last time, and follow up. He effectively showed that he was listening, and he cared.

I also remember walking past him in the corridor one day, and he bothered to say, "hi Andy!" He actually remembered my name!

Not only that, if he knew you were the source of some useful analysis or insight, even if it had been embedded in a presentation by a senior manager, he'd get in touch and say thank you directly.

Those are the kinds of little things I mean.

3. KEEP COMMITMENTS

Keeping commitments is really important when you want to build trust.

And this is probably more a lesson in being careful what commitments we make, so that we know we can stick to them.

The point is, if people come to know you as someone who does what they say they will do, then even your caution in committing to new work becomes a signal that you don't want to let them down. And they start to trust you as someone they can rely on.

4. CLARIFY EXPECTATIONS

Closely related to keeping commitments is clarifying expectations.

I've seen lots of people fall foul of making assumptions.

Sometimes it might be they produce a whole ten-page presentation full of analysis when all the person wanted was a phone call with the answer to a question!

Clearly, we have to be careful we don't go to the extreme of being annoying and clarifying even the blatantly obvious!

But, done well, what this says to the other person is that you care about what they want and why they want it. And if they're going to rely on you to get something done, then you want to be able to do it well.

You can also see it the other way around, when you're delegating. It builds trust when you show that you care that someone succeeds in an activity you've delegated, by being really clear what the expectations are, and by being available and willing to answer questions about it.

5. SHOW PERSONAL INTEGRITY

Showing integrity is important in building trust.

But integrity is more than honesty.

Honesty is telling the truth. Integrity is *being* true.

It means *doing* what we say we're going to do, and *being* the way we know is right.

It means not being hypocritical, for example, complaining about someone cutting corners and then blatantly letting ourselves off for doing the same.

It means not saying, "oh she'll never notice that", while sweeping dust under the rug!

Stephen Covey comments that, "One of the most important ways to manifest integrity is to be loyal *to those who are not present*. In doing so, we build the trust of those who are present."

Even if someone agrees with you when you gossip about someone, if you ever then disagree with them they'll probably think/know that you'll be off gossiping about them to someone else.

Doing the right thing, having personal integrity, builds up trust. Lack of integrity undermines it.

6. APOLOGIZE SINCERELY

When you mess up, if you genuinely apologize this can not only undo the damage to the trust between you and the other person, it can build it up.

A genuine apology means you recognise both the wrong and the impact on the other person.

It means you take ownership and don't try to shift blame.

It means you genuinely care and want to reverse any negative impact.

It means this is not your normal standard.

It means that they can still trust you.

TRUST MAKES THINGS MUCH EASIER IN FINANCE BUSINESS PARTNERING

In the next few chapters we'll start to look at things like negotiating and communicating, but I hope you'll agree that those things become a whole lot easier when there is a foundation of trust.

There are no shortcuts in building trust.

So, decide today what kind of person, what kind of Finance business partner, what kind of CFO, you want to be. And think about what that means for the way that you treat people, and what does that for levels of trust in your relationships.

GREAT CFOS LISTEN WITHOUT PREJUDICE

Communication skills, from lots of viewpoints, are not only something that CFOs benefit from. They're skills for life, and skills for leadership.

That's the same with any of the "personal effectiveness" skills I've written about in the previous chapters. I've directed them towards Finance business partners and CFOs, because those are the people who I hang around with most, professionally.

But, in reality, when we talk about "gravitas" or "maturity", or even "credibility" or "presence" – i.e. the kinds of things that make people listen to you and take you seriously as an adult, rather than a young upstart, all seem to come back to some version of the few things I'm describing as "personal effectiveness".

So, let's have a think about communication skills.

FOUR TYPES OF COMMUNICATION

And let's narrow it down further. There are four types of communication: reading, writing, speaking and listening.

Reading, writing and speaking are abilities and skills that we take for granted in adults, after being taught in school throughout childhood and youth.

And yet, by contrast, listening is something we don't really consider. We kind of just assume that it happens scientifically – sound waves go into our ears and someone's speech registers in our brain!

But that's not really listening. That's hearing!

So, let's talk about the neglected skill of listening...

THE NEGLECTED SKILL OF LISTENING

Penny Ferguson, in her book *Transform Your Life*, refers to a magazine article that was discussing the space shuttle accidents (Columbia and Challenger). It pointed out that both accidents should never have happened because there were people in the organisation that realised what the problems were. "However, nobody was listening to them."

And, I must admit, one of the things I hate the most is being interrupted or talked over (followed closely by being ignored!). But it happens a lot, both at home and at work. It irritates me when people assume they know what I'm going to say before I've completed a sentence, and they either butt in with their own point or their own counterargument (sometimes without me needing to even utter the first word!).

Sometimes I get so fed up of interruptions that I just shut up and wait, and then if I still don't get a chance to get a word in, I mentally disengage. I'm one of those annoying people who leaves a meeting at work silently looking fed up, and then sends an email an hour later. Interruptions can lead to some real dysfunctional behaviour!

Penny Ferguson used to do an exercise with her clients, pairing people up, and asking the listeners to remain silent for 3 minutes (she used a 3-minute hourglass "egg timer") while the other person got to describe how they felt about a topic. They'd then keep swapping round until each person felt that the other person understood all that they wanted to say.

But, simply giving people airtime is not all there is to listening, although it's a massive start.

BAD LISTENING SHOWS IN THE WAY WE RESPOND

There are a couple of ways that our response shows we're not really listening properly.

One way is that we, in Stephen Covey's words, read our autobiography into what someone else says. In other words, we are continually looking for ways to compare our situation with theirs. We'll respond with something like, "oh yeah, that's like when I ...."

You think that you're finding common ground. But in reality, you're twisting their words to fit into your own experience so that you can tell them to simply do what you did.

Another way we don't listen properly is when we decide our response before fully understanding what the other person has to say, even if we wait for them to finish talking. We assume we know what they mean or where their argument is going, and we try to head them off and shortcut the discussion. We prescribe a solution before we've properly diagnosed the problem!

Too much of that will annoy the other person, as you consistently miss their point.

WE SHOULD LISTEN IN ORDER TO UNDERSTAND

Stephen Covey, in *The 7 Habits of Highly Effective People*, says that often we listen to other people in order to respond, rather than listening to understand. But we should, "seek first to understand, then to be understood".

I found this really challenging when I first came across it. I observed myself in the way I was thinking during conversations. And I was shocked. Most of the time while the other person was talking, I was thinking of how to respond. What advice could I give? What examples could I use from my own experience to affirm what they were saying? What was my opinion of what they were saying? I had to be ready to say something in response!

The consequence was that I wasn't really deeply understanding the people I was talking to. And that led to conversations that were superficial, inconclusive or simply dissatisfying.

What we need to do is to *really* listen to the other person.

So, how can we do that?

HOW TO LISTEN TO REALLY UNDERSTAND

Well, here are a few tips taken from Covey's classic book, which can divert us from the need to respond. These are levels we can use in our replies which simply focus on understanding what the other person is trying to communicate. These replies seem really basic, but what they're designed to do is to help us to avoid coming back with our own ideas.

The aim is simply to understand, *really* understand.

So, in the first and most basic level, you can *mimic the content* of what the other person says. If they say, "I don't like Boris Johnson," you reply, "you don't like Boris Johnson."

Notice you don't ask questions. You don't probe or evaluate their statement. You don't say, "is that because you know him personally?" You don't say, "in what sense don't you like him?" You don't ask, "why?" You don't judge the statement and say, "well that's a bit harsh"!

All you're aiming to do is to show that you're paying attention to what they're saying.

At the second level, you *rephrase the content*. So, if someone says, "I don't like Boris Johnson," you could say, "you'd prefer it if Boris Johnson was not Prime Minister in the UK."

This is a little bit better, as it shows you are thinking about what they mean by their initial statement. The thing about this level, though, is that it's quite "left-brained" factual.

Slightly better again, then, at a third level, is *reflecting the feeling* in their statement. So, you might reply, "you're fed up."

The final level is *both rephrasing the content and reflecting the feeling*. So, a reply could be, "you're fed up of the UK government."

The reason this level is best is because it enables the other person to develop both their thoughts and feelings about what they're thinking about. And you haven't asked questions, probed, evaluated their opinions or made any judgment about what they've said.

THE GREAT THINGS ABOUT REALLY LISTENING

In Stephen Covey's words, it's like giving the other person, "psychological air". You're carrying the conversation along in a way that simply gives the other person chance to develop their thinking and feelings, and gives you the chance to listen more deeply and understand.

The fundamental advantage of this kind of listening is that it strengthens your relationship with whoever you're talking with, because they see you as someone who wants to know them and not just work with them or live with them.

I remember being told this about networking. Someone told me that rather than going into a networking event with a prepared "elevator pitch", I should just go prepared to learn about the people I talked to. The irony is that when you make the effort to *just listen* to people, those people go away feeling good about the conversation they've had with you, and see you as a really good person to talk to. In marketing and networking terms, it *makes them want to come back to talk to you again*!

More than that, though, it allows you to have a proper conversation where you respond to what the other person is *actually* saying. And it creates the goodwill where they'll listen to what you have to say.

Sometimes, they may even answer their own questions and solve their own problems in just talking. And that helps them grow and transform at the same time. It also has been known to negate the need for pitching and plugging or "selling". They may say, "I just want to work with someone who understands me."

FINANCE REALLY NEEDS GOOD LISTENERS

And so, you can see how this can be applied to working as a CFO or more generally as a Finance business partner.

As a Finance professional, we have experience, skills and knowledge that can help the business manage its performance so as to perform better. In other words, we have what the business needs to drive performance.

But if we want to provide the right advice, the right solutions, the right guidance, the right leadership, we have to diagnose properly before we prescribe. Therefore, we have to *understand* properly.

Therefore, in Finance we must be fundamentally good listeners.

EVERYONE'S A WINNER WITH GOOD FINANCE BUSINESS PARTNERING

We're accustomed, I think, to talking about a "Win/Win situation" as some scenario where everyone involved in a deal ends up happy with what they got out of it.

I haven't got time to justify (and shouldn't need to anyway) why "Win/Win" is the best outcome to aim for in any relational situation.

But one thing is certain. You don't get Win/Win situations without having a Win/Win mindset.

And when we think of what Finance business partners, CFOs and Finance leaders should be aiming at, it must involve situations where everyone ends as a winner, certainly where the business is concerned.

For instance, as an example scenario, sales managers might feel they have gained some great insight from Finance that will enable them to convert more leads, whilst in the same interaction the Finance manager feels they've got sales managers to better manage risk.

These are the kind of interactions we in Finance want with our non-Finance colleagues. We don't just want our processes and controls to be adhered to because we say so! We want them to be respected because they help our non-Finance colleagues, which helps the business to perform better.

This is what Finance business partnering is all about – not just getting into influential positions for ourselves, but achieving situations where we all win, and therefore the business benefits as a whole.

So, as we're thinking about the personal skills and behaviours that Finance people should develop, this time I want to look at what goes into the Win/Win mindset, and what is needed to achieve results where "everyone's a winner".

IT STARTS WITH CHARACTER

The first thing to realise is that a "Win/Win *mindset*" is not exclusively about negotiating a deal. It's not just the precursor to learning a *technique* for getting a good deal for both sides in a negotiation.

This involves your *philosophy* and the way you see the world.

Most fundamental to this, in my view, is what Stephen Covey calls, the "abundance mindset".

The abundance mindset is a way of looking at the world such that "there is plenty out there and enough to spare for everybody" (from <u>The 7 Habits of Highly Effective People</u>). In the long run, there is no need to rob or cheat someone else to have what we want.

But more than that, our *definition of success* within the abundance mindset is not selfish. We genuinely think in terms of wanting and aiming for positive outcomes *for everyone*, not just ourselves. Quoting Stephen Covey's masterpiece again: "Public Victory does not mean victory *over* other people. It means success in effective interaction that brings mutually beneficial results to *everyone involved*" (emphasis added).

And that definition of success is something that comes from setting our direction in terms of being conscious of our values, and having integrity as we live them out each day. This is what I was trying to say when I wrote about setting the vision and direction earlier.

It's aiming to *be* a certain way (according to our values), rather than *having* or *achieving* certain things.

So, in Finance, it's about balancing our desire to control, to follow due process, or even to have more influence in the business, with the needs of our non-Finance colleagues, so that together we can benefit the business... which makes it an enjoyable place to work, helpful to our customers, caring to our suppliers and profitable for our investors.

BUILD RELATIONSHIPS

When you have a "Win/Win mindset" it becomes natural to build relationships where we genuinely care about the other person's goals as well as our own.

But what if the other person has a different mindset. What if they just want to shut you down? What if they are resistant? What if they want to achieve their objectives with no care for your needs? What if they want to just use you?

If our more important aim is to be mature, to show integrity, to seek the best for everyone, then we will continue to do that even if others don't.

As Stephen Covey says, you continue to show "genuine courtesy, respect, and appreciation for that person and for the other point of view. You stay longer in the communication process. You listen more, you listen in greater depth. You express yourself with greater courage. You aren't reactive. You go deeper inside yourself for strength of character to be proactive. You keep hammering it out until the other person begins to realise that you genuinely want the resolution to be a real win for both of you."

EXAMPLE SITUATIONS

At this point it may be a good idea to have a look at a couple of examples. Because you may be thinking that this is all very well, but not every situation requires "give and take". Sometimes, we are just asked for something by a non-Finance colleague. Sometimes, we have to just ask people to do things. Where does a Win/Win mindset fit in with these situations? What would a Win/Win outcome look like?

Let's say that you are a Finance Manager and you need an Ops Manager to arrange for the collection of some data for some analysis.

Well, if they just do it for you, that's not a Win/Win result. That's a Win/Lose. You've got what you needed at the expense of their time and effort.

A Win/Win mindset would look for some way to ensure that the Ops Manager also got something out of the transaction, or at least had the opportunity to get some sort of benefit from it.

So, perhaps after asking for the data collection you could offer to share the analysis with them and spend some time explaining how it will be used. That would increase their understanding of how business performance is managed, and therefore would benefit both them and the business in the future.

Or perhaps you could simply ask if there's anything you can do for them that would help them out. And if there's nothing that springs to mind right now, assure them of your sincerity to help them out with anything they need in the future.

And what if it was the other way around? What about when the Marketing Manager comes asking for an urgent piece of modelling on a new product that she's working on?

If you just roll your eyes and say you'll fit in the work somehow, even if you're really busy, then you've accepted a Lose/Win outcome, which is not what you want.

To make it a Win/Win, perhaps ask if you can attend a product launch steering committee meeting or join the project team. Then you can learn about what they're doing, and ensure they've thought of everything from a Finance point of view – transaction process, contracts, credit control, data capture, and so on.

I hope you see what I mean.

If you have a pervasive Win/Win mindset, you will always look for ways that you can finish with an outcome that you're all pleased with.

WHERE HARD AND SOFT SKILLS MEET

Here's another example. And this one illustrates how soft skills can impact on the hard technical areas of our role in Finance.

As I've reflected on this from the angle of "personal effectiveness", which is core to the "soft" skills, or behavioural, side of Finance business partnering, I've been struck by how this interacts with one of the thorny issues we have in Finance.

And that's the issue of budgeting!

Stephen Covey says, "Win/Win can only survive in an organisation when the systems support it. If you talk Win/Win but reward Win/Lose, you've got a losing program on your hands."

Traditional budgeting rewards Win/Lose behaviour, because it encourages political "gaming", each manager playing the system to their own ends, with Finance ironically both facilitating and attempting to police the politics!

Win/Win systems tend to be based on clear agreements, delegation, trust and integrity. And that aligns very nicely with the decentralised management methods advocated by the Beyond Budgeting movement.

DEAL-MAKING WHERE EVERYONE'S A WINNER

Finally, let's briefly think about what the process would be in a deal-making situation, where we want to come out with a Win/Win result. This needs to be more of a process. But the process has to align with the mindset.

There are four simple high-level steps in the "everyone's a winner" deal-making process:

1. See the problem from the other point of view. This comes back to the real listening skills I described in the previous chapter. We listen until we really understand what the other party wants and why, and how they are thinking.

2. Identify key issues;

3. Identify what outcome would qualify as fully acceptable to everyone;

4. Come up with new options to achieve those results.

It's not rocket science. But two things are critical:

- *Wanting* a Win/Win outcome, because that's part of your value system;

- *Really listening* because you care about the perspectives, needs and desires of other people, not just yourself.

FINANCE IS ABOUT PEOPLE, NOT NUMBERS

I realise that this kind of thing is not what you expect to find when you read a book within the Finance and Accounting realm!

But, you see, I have this belief that Finance is more about people than it is about numbers.

The numbers would not need to be crunched if they weren't useful for some purpose.

And the purposes are the purposes *of people*!

Numbers don't exist in a vacuum. Different people demand business numbers for different purposes.

So, we'll do our jobs better in Finance if we understand the people, work with the people, and win with the people, who drive the numbers and demand the numbers in the business.

SYNERGIES ARE NOT COST SAVINGS FOR THE BEST CFOS

After qualifying as a Chartered Accountant in public practice in England in 1995, I went to manage a Finance department of 16 people in one of the smaller divisions of a big bank.

It was my first experience of management, which was one of the reasons I took the job. I wanted to learn new skills.

Fortunately for me, at that time the bank was revamping its performance management processes and putting everyone from team leaders to senior executives through new management and leadership training.

And that made me reflect quite deeply on what it meant to manage people and lead teams right from the start of my management career.

One of things I quickly realised was that managers and leaders shouldn't see themselves as delivering personally. It's the team that delivers *together*, not the manager alone.

What that meant for me was that, whilst I had my own individual responsibilities, those responsibilities were secondary to ensuring the required output of my team.

The way I used to explain it was that my purpose as a manager or leader was to make the team "greater than the sum of its parts". I was there to ensure we all pulled in the same direction, had the necessary resources and skills, and worked together effectively.

My involvement as a leader would make us better as a team than if we were just a collection of individuals.

This is the essence of "synergy".

And that's why I think it's unfortunate that when we talk about "synergies" in Finance we quite often think that's synonymous with cost savings. But in reality, that's only the case in one example of synergy – where there's an overlap of activity in a business combination.

I also think it's unfortunate that when people read Stephen Covey's classic book, *The 7 Habits of Highly Effective People*, they often dismiss his sixth habit – *Synergize* – as something mystical and inaccessible.

My view is that when we see someone we consider to be a great leader, what they've achieved is the ability to "synergize", to create synergy, to make things greater than the sum of the parts. Great leaders make us feel we're an important part of something, that we have a great purpose, that we're trusted and valued, that the team would miss us if we weren't there, that working together is the key to achieving things.

It's also probably what we'd most likely relate to the term "gravitas". Have you ever read a job advert for a senior role that asks for "gravitas" or "presence"? It used to really frustrate me! What the heck do they mean? How can they test for it? Surely, it's just one of those things you know when you see it, but you couldn't describe it?

What I've come to see is that if you want to have the "gravitas" to be in Finance leadership and business leadership, you need to aim for synergy.

So, in this chapter we're going to look at *how* you can achieve that. What do you need to do? How do you need to think, and to be, in order to bring about synergy, to make things greater than the sum of the parts?

1 – ENCOURAGE A CAN-DO ATTITUDE

Firstly, to encourage synergy, you have to somehow imbue a can-do attitude into the group, into the individuals involved.

In a previous chapter I explained that the foundation for personal effectiveness is a "can-do attitude".

A can-do attitude recognises that all human beings, ourselves included, have the ability to learn, to make decisions, to recognise right and wrong, to use our imagination. We are not animals governed by deterministic or mechanistic responses. We can *choose* what we do and how we respond to a larger extent than we normally give ourselves credit for.

I used to say to my team in that bank, using the Henry Ford quote, "if you think you can or think you can't, you're right!"

A few years later, as a Finance Director, I was criticised by one of my managers for having my "head in the clouds". That was because as we were trying to plan our way through a really difficult juggling act of high priority projects and business-as-usual, I refused to give up trying to find the best solution. I didn't let the situation get me down. I just kept asking questions to consider different angles.

The foundation for synergizing is helping people to believe that in the situation in question, and in general, they have choice, that their imagination and conscience are valuable, and that their thoughts are a valuable contribution.

2 – LISTEN WELL AND REALLY CARE WHAT OTHER PEOPLE THINK

Earlier I stressed the importance of listening – *really* listening – to people.

And when I say *really* listening, I mean listening with the purpose of *understanding* the other person, not just to work out how to answer them.

It's being open and really valuing other people and their perspectives.

If you are trying to find a solution to a problem, why would you believe that you alone have all the best ideas? Can you really be confident that you've considered every aspect and every angle?

You already know what you think. Getting *someone else's* thoughts gives you new information, helps you get more insight, learn new things.

And, has it ever crossed your mind that the people you meet are so much deeper than what you get to see each day?

You may see someone at work every day, working in a particular way. But then if you saw them at home with their kids and their hobbies, you'd say things like, "you're a completely different person at home!" Or, "I never knew you had such a creative talent for artwork," or whatever.

We also can't see the experiences people have had that can influence their thinking. Someone may have learnt valuable life lessons from an accident, serious illness, bereavement, mistakes, relationship problems. It's not necessarily that people hide these things. It's often that there's no need or no time to talk about them.

When you *really* listen to people you give them what Stephen Covey calls, "psychological air". You give them space to develop their thinking and to explain what influences their thinking from things they've learnt and experiences they've had.

And this contributes to synergy because it allows you to see more aspects of the problem you're trying to solve or the question you're trying to answer.

It's like shooting a film with multiple camera angles. The more angles you have, the richer and more authentic you can make the experience for the audience.

3 - BUILD TRUST

Another important thing you need in order to generate synergy when you bring people together is trust.

When people trust each other, they are more willing to listen, and more willing to make themselves vulnerable by sharing undeveloped thinking. And that can often lead to powerful new ideas when people help one another to think things through.

I talked about this earlier. And I outlined the kind of things that build trust – taking time to understand people, not neglecting the small things, keeping commitments, clarifying expectations, showing personal integrity, apologizing sincerely when necessary.

These things take time. Trust isn't something that turns up overnight based on following some simple technique.

And this is why, as predominantly left-brained accountants, we shouldn't dismiss or avoid team building events or the embarrassing "ice breakers" in workshop sessions.

And this is why we should be careful and respectful and mature in the way that we treat *all* people, *every* day of our lives, in *every* situation.

Taking time and effort to treat people right, as fellow human beings, every day, will pay dividends when we really need synergy in situations in the future.

4 - BELIEVE THAT BETTER SOLUTIONS COME FROM COLLABORATION

The other thing that contributes to making 1+1 = more than 2 (which is simply saying that we're making more than the sum of the parts, the definition of synergy) is a win/win mindset.

Again, I've explained before that a win/win *mindset* is a fundamental belief rather than a negotiating stance or technique.

And this is something that is genuinely hard to get used to.

I mean, when you go to a workshop session, what are you normally thinking beforehand?

Well, if you're anything like me, you're probably thinking how you're going to share your views on the subject and how you can persuade people to come round to your way of thinking!

A win/win mindset looks at things differently. It goes into the workshop wondering what interesting new perspectives we're going to encounter. And it believes that the final solution will be something that no one has thought of beforehand, but is something that is better than anyone could have thought of on their own.

This interacts with the aspect of trust, in that when you trust that others also want the same thing, and when you believe that they also want to find the best solution possible, then you're more willing to adjust or give up the view you came in with.

The interesting thing is that when trust is low, you may be willing to *compromise*. This is giving up something for the sake of something else. In this case, however, *everybody* loses something. It's not win/win. It's $1+1 = $ less than 2!

When trust is high you all truly believe that by collaboration, and by understanding everyone's positions fully, you will find a *new* solution that better fits *all* the requirements rather than just some of them. And it will be better than anything that any one person could have come up with on their own.

SYNERGIZING FINANCE LEADERSHIP

So, what has this all got to do with Finance business partnering and CFOs? What has this got to do with Finance leadership?

Well, I guess the immediate application is within our teams and within the Finance department itself.

Collaborative, consultative, synergistic thinking will pay dividends at any level, whether you're a team member, a team leader, a manager or a senior Finance leader or executive.

And as you cultivate this way of thinking more and more, you will mature and make yourself ready for increasing levels of responsibility, and therefore increasing seniority. You will attain that "gravitas" that the job adverts talk about!

But it also applies to the way that we deal with our non-Finance colleagues and departments.

Do we really believe that improving the interaction – the synergy - between Finance and the rest of the business can make the business better? Can the business as a whole be greater than the sum of its parts (of which Finance is just one part)?

Can we create synergistic ways of working with our non-Finance colleagues, where we seek to understand them first before trying to help them; where we build trust with them by keeping commitments, not undermining their work, finding ways to make them more successful; where we demonstrate that we believe in collaboration and not simply political influence?

Surely, this is the pinnacle of purpose-driven Finance and business-focused Finance.

HAPPY AND EFFECTIVE CFOS TAKE CARE OF THEMSELVES

Probably the most important thing to recognise as you develop in your career (and in your life) is that *continued progress takes continued effort*.

It's not one-dimensional, either. Many people think – and I'm applying this to Finance people, but it can equally apply to anyone – that continued development is just a case of learning more stuff. We learn accounting, pass accounting exams, and then we progress in our careers by learning more stuff about accounting. Wrong!

Or, worse, we believe that once we've got the qualification then it's just a case of accumulating years and automatically going on up the ladder. Nope! It doesn't happen like that!

No, to be "the best version of you" you need to attend to *four dimensions*. And I'll come on to those in a minute.

And the other element that is important in personal and career development is *intentionality*. Making effort, even if balanced in the four dimensions, will get you so far. But without intention – in other words, without knowing what you're aiming at or what you want to achieve – your progress will be random and patchy.

So, what I'm going to present in this chapter is hopefully enough of a flavour to get you going, bearing in mind that whole books are written about this one topic!

And talking about books, let me right away mention two. Try and get these two books and read them (preferably more than once). If you put what you learn into practice, it will change your life. And I am not exaggerating!

First, Stephen Covey's *7 Habits of Highly Effective People*.

Second, Jim Loehr and Tony Schwartz's *The Power of Full Engagement*[11].

THE FOUR DIMENSIONS

Both of the two books I'm recommending speak about the makeup of human nature in the same way. We are made up of these four dimensions: spiritual, mental, social/emotional and physical.

The *physical* side is kind of obvious – exercise, nutrition, (physical) strength, stamina, etc.

The *spiritual* side is your core, your value-system. It's the dimension that controls all the others, because it holds your priorities, your desires, your likes and dislikes, your moral compass.

The *mental* dimension is about clarity, (mental) strength, dealing with stress, and using all of our brain's capability and not just some

---

[11] The UK title of this book is "On Form".

of it (e.g. not just being analytical, but showing imagination and intuition).

And the *emotional/social* side of our nature is about the quality of our relationships, how well we live in our communities as interdependent human beings, and the cultivation of positive rather than negative emotions (e.g. happiness rather than anxiety or anger).

IT'S ABOUT ENERGY, NOT TIME

The quality of the way we live our lives, or the personal effectiveness that I've been talking about in this book, is a function of the amount of energy we have in each of those four dimensions.

We all know this deep down. However good we are at planning our calendars and scheduling our days, if we are tired because we've been "out on the razz" the night before (or binge-watching Netflix TV series'), we'll tune out of the 9am strategy meeting and we'll be ineffective.

Likewise, if we're in the middle of a text message battle with our spouse and he/she's just told you they won't be there when you get home... just as you're trying to write an important report... you'll be too distracted and upset to concentrate.

It doesn't matter how much time you put into things, or how much time you have available, if you haven't got the right amount of physical, spiritual, emotional and mental energy, you won't do the best you can.

What we need are ways of ensuring that each dimension is able to give us the right amount of energy at the right time to make us more effective in every sphere of our lives. Stephen Covey calls this "sharpening the saw". Jim Loehr calls it "energy management".

The phrase, "sharpening the saw", comes from the story that Covey uses to illustrate the importance of taking time for intentional energy management or "self-renewal".

He pictures a lumberjack trying to cut down a tree with a blunt saw, and it's taking him all day.

Someone comes along and says, "you'd get that done a lot quicker if you sharpened your saw."

The lumberjack replies, "I haven't got time to sharpen the saw! I've got to get this tree cut down!"

Absurd, isn't it, when put like that? But we pretty much all do it every day in different ways to some extent.

So, here, very briefly, are Jim Loehr's principles for managing energy more effectively:

1. We should draw on all four sources of energy – physical, emotional, mental and spiritual;

2. We need to intentionally balance energy expenditure with energy renewal;

3. To build increased capacity in any of the dimensions we must push ourselves intentionally beyond our normal limits;

4. Positive energy rituals (or habits) help to give us consistent and sustained high performance.

I've spoken enough about the first point already. So, here's the way we should be thinking about the others.

ENERGY EXPENDITURE NEEDS TO BE BALANCED WITH ENERGY RENEWAL

The key insight under this heading comes from using the physical dimension as a guide to the way that energy management works.

What I mean by that is that we know that, in order to have the physical energy to spend on what we want to do, we have to have bodies that have that energy.

And, given that our energy is reduced throughout each day by spending it on what we want to do, we need to renew our energy each day.

Physically, our energy renewal comes from eating right (foods that build energy rather than deplete it), exercising to give us physical strength and stamina, and through recognising a rhythm of work and rest.

The work/rest rhythm, in particular, is an interesting one.

Physically, we can think of it in terms of getting enough sleep each day and balancing working days with holidays and weekends.

But, the same applies in the other dimensions. Just like running for eight hours would leave us physically worn out and probably broken, mentally focusing on the same task for hours makes us mentally exhausted.

We need to take regular mental breaks, which can mean switching off or just switching to a different kind of task.

Socially and emotionally, too, we can spend emotional energy being there for people and getting the best out of people. Perhaps we can renew that energy through spending time *away from* people, reflecting on how we can better understand people or work for win/win situations.

Spiritually, we renew our energy by regaining our clarity of purpose, through spending time reconnecting with our values, our personal mission, and our deepest reasons for doing things.

Daily grind often pushes our values and purpose into our subconscious, and we lose the power of that energy source. So, we need to take time out to bring them back to the forefront of our minds, and to continue to work out their implications in our lives.

WE CAN INCREASE OUR CAPACITY BY DELIBERATELY PUSHING OURSELVES

Again, this principle comes from observing the way that physical capacity is developed.

When you want to get physically stronger, or fitter, or to get more stamina, you would do training.

Each training session you would do a little more, and then a little more, and build up – the weight you can lift, the efficiency of your heart, the time/distance you can keep going.

The thing is that you don't build up if you're not regularly pushing past your existing limits. Bodybuilders build muscle by lifting more than their muscles can cope with. They, believe it or not, cause their muscles to tear slightly. The body then self-heals (during the recovery/renewal phase) and the muscles end up stronger, because the body recognises it needs that new capacity.

Note: that means that good physical training always pushes past a pain barrier. It always hurts. (Remember Adam Sandler in *Happy Gilmour*, standing in front of the automatic baseball thrower at close range trying to toughen himself up?!)

The same is true in the mental dimension, where we seek to always stretch the limits of what we understand, learn new skills, etc.

And in terms of mental strength, we push ourselves past failures which hurt.

And you could also think about exercising your creative skills, your analytical skills, and so on, by intentionally trying to apply them in new and increasingly complex areas.

You get the picture?

BUILDING RITUALS AND HABITS WILL HELP US CONTINUE TO IMPROVE

And just as muscles lose tone, and the body loses fitness, through lack of physical exercise, unless we're regularly "sharpening the saw" across all four dimensions we will see our "production capability" steadily reducing instead of growing.

The thing is that maintaining focus on spend/renewal, getting the right exercise, across four dimensions of human nature, is quite complex unless you have a system.

What we need are habits and rituals that mean that we don't have to overthink (spending mental and spiritual energy) by rethinking every day the way we manage our energy.

There are so many helpful things that can be said about making new rituals for ourselves and changing our habits, but we don't have space in this chapter to go deep.

So, what can I helpfully say in the remaining space?

In Stephen Covey's terms, habit forming is a process of "making and keeping commitments" to ourselves and others. There's an "upward spiral" of renewal that continually goes through the cycle of "learn – commit – do".

But let's be realistic. New Year's resolutions are effectively new habits that we want to introduce into our lives. Most of them fail to stick. Why?

I wrote an article on my personal blog[12] about what I learnt from my quest to regain physical fitness during my recovery from cancer treatment. That has some very relevant observations. But there are two that are worth focusing on here:

First, don't try to do too much too soon. Start embarrassingly small!

When I started using an exercise bike to get fitter, I did just 10 minutes and just over 2km (virtually) on the first day. I barely broke a sweat any day in the first week or so. But, I was then able to do more each day (which was motivating), and I got used to what the pain barrier felt like. After a couple of weeks, I was into the habit, and only a few weeks later I was doing five times more virtual distance and three times more time.

Don't be afraid to start small. It's amazing how quickly small incremental gains mount up into something impressive.

---

[12] http://andyburrows.me/getting-physical/

Second, you have to *really* want the result, and really *believe* that your new habits will get you that result.

What got me on the exercise bike day after day even when my body complained I was overdoing it?

It was the desperate desire to be able to do the physical things I've done in the past – distances I've walked without getting tired, weights I've been able to lift, etc. And that was coupled with the belief (from experience) that habitually pushing past my limits and then allowing recovery would slowly but surely increase my physical capacity.

Many people give up on new habits and resolutions because they either try to do too much too quickly, or they haven't given themselves chance to prove their habits work, or they just don't really want the result enough to justify the inevitable pain barriers.

CONCLUSION

To conclude, I just want to reemphasise that unless we're regularly taking time to intentionally work on what Covey calls our "production capability" it will shrink rather than grow.

If we're not moving forwards, we'll be moving backwards. Perhaps slowly and imperceptibly. But at some stage, when you find yourself exhausted, or grouchy, depressed or disconnected, you'll realise that lack of exercise or lack of balance (either spend/renewal balance or balance across the four dimensions) has led you there.

Have a think about which areas of your life are struggling for energy. And think about what habits and rituals you can introduce into your life to keep you in a "virtuous circle". And don't be afraid to start small and tentative...

... but do *keep going*!

ABOUT THE AUTHOR

Andy Burrows is a popular Finance writer, coach and online trainer.

He qualified as a Chartered Accountant in England in 1995, and has worked in business Finance since 1996, with the likes of Barclays, Centrica, Logica, and Zurich Insurance.

Having experienced a wide variety of Finance roles, including Finance Director, and having played key roles in both Finance and business transformation programmes, Andy increasingly spends his time passing on the benefit of his wealth of experience.

As Founder and CEO of **Supercharged Finance**[13], he provides online training and development opportunities and material to help Finance professionals get better at helping the businesses they work for.

---

[13] www.superchargedfinance.com

Made in the USA
Columbia, SC
26 February 2021